Recovery

Writing on Air Anthology 2024

ISBN: 978-1-913122-64-5

Cover image: Martyn Wilson at Hardwired

Cover design: Mike Farren

Typesetting: Mike Farren

Editing: Peter Spafford and Mike Farren

RECOVERY – an introduction

Welcome to the 2ⁿᵈ Chapel FM Writing On Air anthology, this year themed around the idea of Recovery. In case you missed (the theme was Missing) our first anthology and haven't come across us before, Chapel FM is an arts centre in Seacroft, Leeds, housing a live venue, cafe and rehearsal space along with a vibrant radio station, East Leeds Community Radio. Writing On Air is an annual celebration of words and ideas broadcast in its entirety on ELCR.

As a cultural and community centre we work with many individuals both in our local East Leeds locale and throughout Leeds, but we also love to collaborate with organisations who share our democratic, participatory ethos; from LS14, Kentmere Community Centre and SCOT in Seacroft through to The British Library and The National Poetry Centre, both national organisations soon to plant bricks and mortar in the heart of our city.

Chapel FM is a hub for all kinds of writers and writing groups and this anthology brings together work from a great many of them: Chapel FM Writing Group, our own young writers plus others from Leeds East Academy; Orb in Knaresborough, WordPlay, Wordship, Yaffle's Nest, as well writers from our twin city Dortmund in Germany. Just like our lovely building during the Writing On Air festival, this book bustles with poets and fiction writers, some widely published, others in print here for the first time.

Thanks to Leeds Philosophical and Literary Society and Leeds East Academy for supporting the publication; to Yaffle Press and editor Mike Farren for once again making it a reality, and finally to all the writers who have contributed their fabulous writing to this anthology.

Peter Spafford, Director of Words, Chapel FM Arts Centre.

Thanks also to poet Emma Storr for her careful reading and sifting of the submitted work. 'I really enjoyed reading the contributions on this Recovery theme. There was such a range of creative and impressive work and so many different interpretations of the topic, from personal health issues to global concerns, like climate change. Some writers wrote in rhyme while others produced prose poems or free verse, and I'm sure a sonnet or two found their way into the mix. Thank you for giving me this opportunity.'

Contents

Therapy and shoes

The church of our remembering is as deep as any mine, darker than a fairy tale forest. Our days are glass-sharp, crystal-splinters of light slicing the canopied gloom. They're a startled owl rising, a scuffle of shrews, a mangled, bloody fox who comes bellying, a sinuous weasel or some renegade polecat, slinking through the rain-sodden loam.

With no compass to guide us and landmarks being few, we find ourselves journeying in circles. Then we ask ourselves: *What is it we seek? How, if we could choose, would we be saved?* But we, my heart and I, know full well we must learn to be our own magic beanstalk / talking cat /seven league boots / pink fairy with three wishes and a wand.

We may find our redemption in the trail we laid but no woodsman with an axe will come to save us. We are searching for that place where we missed our step, after which we lost our way.

Sometimes we will question if it's all to any purpose. *Isn't this a self-defeating exercise?* We've travelled too far from our point of departure. Nothing now can be changed. But our aim is not to alter the past, only to know how it happened. So many miles we've stumbled in cramped, ill-fitting shoes. They pinched us till we bled. Now we'll climb aboard our carpet and we'll fly.

Abigail Ottley

Self-portrait with acupuncture needle

I have adopted the pose
of a crusader knight:
hands folded, feet crossed.
The needle quivers, an arrow
between my brows.
Hic Harold Rex interfectus est.

By rights, my cat should be here,
curled on my chest in posture of fidelity.
But she is otherwise engaged,
inhabiting elsewhere
the pleasures of her liquid body,
the obsessions of her walnut brain.

Adrian Salmon

Peach pit

The walls of reality are stretched thin,
veins pulsing, gums red,
mottled stitches criss-crossing,
leaving a cosmic hole,
a vacuum ready to encase
like I am a peach pit
within an ill fitting skin,
my true wants and desires
hidden from even me,
a sticky orbit,
juices slather skin
– I wish to remove –
Spit out the core of me.
I will not be contained.
I will spill over.
The pit may grow into a tree.

Alex Callaghan

Can I still catch you?

I can count all the marriages
we've had inside this one,
each leaving a trace.

The lines in our faces
find slipped
time: the first moment
you caught me,
your black polo neck,
goatee beard;
the long middle years,
our son, my mum, your dad.

We're somewhere new,
your mind can't recover
places and names.
I correct you,
sometimes.

Ali Murphy

Filling up the space

So many books, papers and objects
Imprison me in my home.
Unable to sort or throw things away
Decisions too hard to make.

My husband used to throw things out
He didn't share my point of view
What mattered to him was space
I mourned my lost possessions.

Now I've got so many things
I can play with them all day
Sewing, painting, reading
I've got everything I need.

Angie Smiles

Sweetest hangover

You might not think so now but you will *get over it.*

Maddy knew her Mum was trying to be helpful, but really...? Too many cliches. Then as if on cue:

Plenty more fish in the sea.

Mum, please get out of my bedroom.

Maddy watched her Mum back towards the door wearing a slightly wounded expression.

Why can no-one understand? I don't want to get over it. She took herself back to the Maddy of three months ago. Before that her life was a blank. Empty. Then HE came along. Suddenly she could feel. She was ALIVE. Every nerve in her body tingled. Every minute counted.

She started scrolling through the photos. Hundreds of them.

So what if he was moving away? Melbourne wasn't that far. The point was, she was loved. Not in the way your parents love you. They have no choice. This was special. And she would love him back, forever. That's real love.

What was that record her Mum played every time she turned the kitchen into a disco?

If there's a cure for this, I don't want it.

That Ross woman was right. She would not let go of this. No way.

Madeleine, come and get your dinner, you've got to eat.

Maddy opened her mouth to say, one more time, that she wasn't hungry, but then...

She looked at her screensaver, at the face she would never forget, rolled off the bed, shoved the phone in her pocket and clumped downstairs.

Ann Clarke

All clear

This woman I am now
walks the path beside
the black canal.

She thinks *wine-dark, wine-dark*
in rhythm with two sticks
that take turns with her feet
to drag through gravel.

She thinks *chimera,*
pieced from body parts,
soldered with slow poison,
vomit, sweat, tears
of stomach lining.

She thinks *shape-shifter,*
bent around herself,
skin sloughed, hair gone
and so much weight
there are holes around her
that hogweed, knotweed, balsam
distort themselves to fill.

She thinks *hag,*
acolyte, a bald old woman
sightful in the water.
She will slip her tablets,
bargain with Minerva
for what was stolen,
with Apollo for sudden time
and what comes next.

This woman I am now
moves slow as the canal.
She thinks there is a bridge,
somewhere,
a road away.
She is not there yet.

Ann Heath

Untitled IV

spring is soo waylocked out save the spring.
who hurls words in Aristophanes breath.
as the milk curdled disaffected health.
a death so regular no one blinks, no
not one person. the critter of bells
that toll to clanging as the actors
take to the floor tiles wily and
swaay, the way these hordes
march in my dreams, I am
a general or a dead man.
where are blessings on
the cheek that make
men weak at the
knees. Weekly
I pray for a, a
revelation.
but no, no
one else
is pra
ying,
with
me.

Aqeel Parvez

A fallen writer's philosophy

I am the tissue
Of a fallen writer's philosophy;
A product of his trials, tribulations,
Joys, and jubilations.
His experience channels through my flesh-
His soul irrigates my mind.
I am his unwithered remains.

Yet, years away,
I hear the faint whirring
Of a pulping machine-
Designed to macerate my existence.

The tearing of my grain-paper
Will pierce my eardrums
And that pain, that agony-
It will leak down my lobes,
Trace the path to my jugular,
Penetrate the tenderest region of my skin
There, I am slain,
Without recompense, without mercy.

The strenuous recovery
Of my fragmented carcass
Occurs inevitably and I,
That fallen writer's philosophy,
Am reborn, in literature.

Such is the fate of any writer's word.

Benjamin T. Grunwell

The repair shop

Today, on a special time-travel edition of The Repair Shop, we go back to the late 1960s, where Jay tries to fix something for Paul McCartney...

So, Paul, what seems to be the problem, mate?

Well, I'm fixing a hole where the rain gets in...

Oh, that seems like a straightforward job...

Well, not exactly. You see, it's to stop my mind from wondering where it will go...

Oh, well, in that case, I think you might want to see a psychiatrist...

I don't think that'll be necessary, actually. The problem just seems to be getting better all the time. You see, I used to get mad at my school...

Yeah, I don't need your life story, mate!

Next time, on the second part of this time-travel edition of The Repair Shop, we take a trip forward into the early 1970s, where Jay tries to mend something for Barry Gibb...

So, Barry, what can I do for you?

Well, Jay, I was just wondering... How can you mend a broken heart?

Sorry, mate, I don't work miracles!

Billy Myers

A stripped theatre

Is it forty-four decades ago
Staring down these steep stained stairs
I knew my glow was gone – it was
Everything which left me to depreciate
Is all I had learnt to love and admire,
My mind is spinning thinking about all the struggle
All my highs and lows
The foundation which lay unshaken unmoved
Filled with concrete and cement
Toughened and strengthened

The tides were record high
The night slipped away under my watch
I witnessed the last sparks of cheer and laughter

I could bear no more fruits
So I had no profit or great avail to them
My curtains tore apart like a page
The stage went ablaze engulfed in a flame
Showcasing the worst tragedy of my crumbling lifetime
A series of choruses throughout my body – a theatre on fire
So poetic yet so chaotic

I look over the horizon each day
I admire the shining stars
Remembering I was once one
Sometimes I get to see the northern lights
Taking me back to the seamless scenes forty-four decades ago
When all living creatures big and small
Saw a vibrant theatre with lively performances
A home to all creative minds

I never thought such an icon would change
There's little I could do back then
There's nothing I can do now
There's still a scope of hope in a distance
Regeneration, a better reputation
For, once a building's derelict,
Nothing will ever remain the same

Bryan Jayden Muzambi

Missing

This is a day of missing
Deep missing for all the people I have lost
They swim around in my soul
Float like feathers in my blood
Today they can fill my heart
I was at one time afraid of such feelings
The tsunami of grief I felt after daddy left the world
His absence was a huge hole
I did not know him
And had to stitch his pieces into my heart
Carefully for years after
Tiny little stitches that still pull from time to time

Mum when you passed
You turned August into an empty cavern
Of grief
Forays to Fewston
flowers and family
Filled the house
As we waited for her funeral
In the new darkness of evenings
Enjoyed in quiet cups of tea

Today I have come home to myself
To sit in this house that feels empty
The last to leave
A beautiful Ukranian girl
And though it was all I ever wanted for her
I miss her routine
Her quiet patterings
Around the house
Even her deep resentment of my naughty cat

Who drove her to distraction
Every day

Most of all I miss you my friend
Our paths crossed briefly
And under the dark stars
You lit my heart
You said we were connected by past, present and future
But I do not have enough trust in me to hold this
And I know that in the missing of you
I am finding the lost parts of myself
And though I cry as I write this poem
I am not afraid
Of this deep loss
That is healing me
For surely this is the loss
That can heal the world

Carmel Gibbons

Becoming reconciled

Touched by the intentions of too many
Unasked for advice given too freely
Many hands make light work

But not for me
Confusion set in

Retreat
Go back inside
Find the essence
With select company

Trusting the thoughts now of a few
Mingled with my own view
Like my pinguicula I develop anew
Like a phoenix rises from the damage
I rise again from my centre
The core a new growth
Shedding the old

Outwards
Stepping out and in my own time
Learning as I go

Catherine Lynne Kirkby

Untitled

The object sits upon a counter, cracked and worn.
Its shell which once shone brightly has now chipped and dulled,
Its shining lustre long-since faded and its gleam no longer did tout.
A trophy once displayed proudly now marked by both soot and flame,
disguising noble charm beneath a crust of barren embers long burned
out.

This is not to say that its grandeur has too been reduced simply to
dross,
It stands as a memento far too steeped in the history of a family for
such ignoble end.
And so it sits, perched on a stand, behind the magnifier, alone on a
craftsman's bench,
under the dense glow of the limelight that all this time it has forgone.

With hope to once become that jewel on the proverbial crown that was
the mantlepiece.
Its throne beckons for it to sit once where it did beside Picture and
Chain.
Both too were relics of history passed, which displayed proudly, served
to fulfil a promise.
To still remember, and never forget, those who have gone ahead before
us.

Though now the object lies in pieces that is not to say that the memory
does too.
For each fragment will get its time, each half remembered story told to
those who remain.
Cleaned, polished, and set in place amid every other fragment of
meaning carefully pieced.
Until finally, its whole now returned, and into place all the parts of a
mechanism once lost.

So those who hold it now might now feel the tick... of time passing
once more.

Chalky The Punk

An ode to bed

Wherever you lay your head, there I am.
But upstairs in four walls is usually where I lie.
And you lie on me.
And sometimes in me.
Illuminated by soft lamps and harsh rectangle screens.
There I am.

You leave this world here
In mind, not body.
For I am a portal to another realm.
And in my sheets, life is often created.
I am a miracle maker.
But you never even notice.

Chris O'Connor

What we bring back with us – each their own detectorist

Time can be unkind
as we lose our older tongue
Selig Suffolk – **Silly** Suffolk.
Holy changed to **daft**.

Now recovering the spirit of Sutton Hoo
we are seen as sad men of modern Suffolk,
searching for our ancestors' spoor
we troop out each weekend
scrabble for the droppings
on the stable plain
and in the folds of rolling hills,

we seek out the carelessly disregarded,
or the tragic loss
of a dead wife's brush, her brooch.
We comb history for comfort
as much as treasure in the domestic,

find what we need to.

Colin Day

Travelling with heart

We've booked the Festival
at Essakane, north of Timbuktu

paid for visas, flights, injections,
bumpy weeks in 4X4s.

And we're pacing our damp garden path
considering this new revelation

of your heart, now one with special needs:
beta-blockers, statins, surgery after Christmas.

Should we stay
within reach of Cardiology?

*

You might have thought too long,
let fear police you in dreams,

instead, determined as a pilgrim,
you surrendered to your path.

All the way from Bamako
you paced yourself, taking your time,

even lagging behind,
asking for help with your bags.

And this was new to me, to know you
listening so closely to your heart.

*

The Tuareg men, tall in turbans
sit silently on camels,

a living palisade
between dancing and desert.

The women flow
in rippling circles of indigo.

Guitar riffs dazzle
the Saharan stars.

Warm in camel blankets, we
rest in the heartbeat of drums.

*

After the angiogram
the surgeon pale with shock:

quadruple stents
at least, no guarantees.

Still glowing from our journey,
you talk, as if to reassure him,

of the endless desert
the stars at Essakane.

Cora Greenhill

One day, someday

How did one day at a time turn into not the right time?
How did one day turn into someday?
How did that day turn into yesterday and yesterday?

How did it's not the right time
Turn into doing time?

How did my life turn around
leaving me inside out on the inside of the inside of the inside of me?

I was in prison, in a prison, and the prison was still me,
and maybe that is what it means to tell someone you love
you are not the things they hoped you would be

When did you cast a shadow on all the wrongs you can't make right?
Turn a day into a night
a night into a day, just to say I tried

What does it take when every day is too late to say I am sorry?
When words are but a story, you tell yourself to move on
How often that is all a day can bring
Who waves the white flag and shouts forgive me?

How did *you will never be anything* turn into all your dreams and
        more?
How can you learn to love yourself and stop keeping score?
One day, not today, just one day, someday, you'll get it right

Dalton Harrison

Recovering
(for Igshaan Adams)

From South Africa to Yorkshire solstice
past barbs and entanglements
intricate ties,
and lures,
concatenations,
you're bringing back your earlier
making of forms, and former
life-times
of flexed hands twisting and fingers'
forethought
through sandstorms
to set them free in the billowing clouds and nebulae of your sculpture;
the traces where dancers' bodies
touched the floor
inscribe themselves inside your tapestries,
the stitching of interstitial
things, circles, skewed rings,
communities teasing
strands, flotsam, wire
re-covering,
still seem to spin as if a living being
whirls loose in the web, recovering a sense
of threading air with intricate incursions,
the atmosphere's molecular furniture
mapped from the refuse-heaps and
cast-off re-cycled
jewellery of stars upturned
Alpha to Proxima Centauri
your dark blue altocumulus
flickers a tensile lightning
of inner chemistry

against the answer
of inner eye

and you separate, a sudden, walking out
now beyond the mesh unsnared
and unabated, turning through and through your selves -
instanter satellite.

David Annwn

Before I was born

A Brecon farmer turned miner
left the lark and curlew,
congregations of rooks
and hills flocked with sheep.

Wrapped both hands around a pick
lifted a shovel, dug a new life
of muck and darkness choking him daft,
good Welsh coal spewed out of his pit
to feed every Dreadnought's furnaces.

Just as tired, just as filthy
but with dust, not slurry and dung,
he sat in his bath, the fire alive,
saw bread and cheese on his table
not the empty bones of his father's hunger.

David Harmer

Morphine dream

I often fantasise about
Being back in
Sheffield Hallamshire hospital
When I was ill
Not for the pain
Although it did feel good to feel
Or the toilet mishaps
Or the I can't breathe
Or the not being able or allowed to eat
Or the not being able to wash myself
Or the I can't speak
Or the I can't communicate
Please understand me
Or the I can't colour in the lines
Please hold me
Or the I have too many visitors at a time
Or the vomiting
Or the shitting
Or the ogling
No

I miss that hospital window
And brushing my hair with one hand for hours
And being clapped to reach the toilet
Because it's perhaps the last time
I'd ever not feel the unrelenting need
To be productive

The steady ebb and flow of the machines beeping
A tenacious consolation prize of peace and quiet
Maybe I didn't win but at least I didn't die
When they released me
I didn't realise
I'd never be alone again
And by alone I mean
Not with my emails

Eleanor May Blackburn

For when you are lost

look up
look at the sky
they are the stars you know,
perhaps a symbol
a life once lived,
they shine quite bright tonight,
set against
desperation,
pain,
hate,
a glimpse of a memory,
laughter and the sweet sound of family,
a golden haze,
once forgotten,
but not forgotten forever,
time can take a toll on us
down here on earth,
but sometime,
somewhere,
remember the stars,
you need not explain.

Ellie Thompson

A Wish

I wish I could repair you.
I wish I could take you into my workshop,
Set you down among the broken pieces of machinery,
And repair the damage you suffered.
I wish I could take you apart and put you back together in better
       condition.
What use are these hands,
What good are my skills,
If I can't use them to help you?
I wish I could repair you.
And then maybe
You could repair me too.

Emmy

Missing on the Remarkables

Search will resume at first light.

In the hotel room
she must pack
try to pack for him
needs his padlock code

three numbers
part history date

by two am
she has a system
rotates numbers
like rosary beads

at four am
numbers
makes tea

light at seven
numbers
hears the helicopter

seven thirty the lock clicks open
066

simple then

eight thirty the phone rings
spotted in a gully
rescue on
coming down

she packs his things

Gail Mosley

The lost, is to be found

go
go on
go find the hidden
reclaim that which was
that, state of mind
that, state of being
that, state of truth

go from your shade
go on
go into sparkling illumination
stride outward
and inward
onward with haste
with intent
with love
for others
of others
and of yourself

go, be free
go on
go because you need
that missing piece
that sacred peace.

Gareth Rhodes

Revelled in your company

I can tell you exactly how long it has been since I last revelled in your
company.
Just the two of us, anticipation and trepidation on the menu.
This was to be a last supper, steeped in biblical ramifications,
drowned in the blood of Christ.

God did I drown.

Sinking, trying to catch a breath, my last thought was of you.
I surfaced amongst a fog of memories distilled down the ages.
A familiar sour taste of regret clung to my stained teeth, laminating my
tongue like velvet tarmac.
By then you were gone, absent, absconded.

The monotone sky of the new day, of the new year, was the perfect hue
of surrender,
I hid my intent next to a box of hope that had long been buried in a
concrete garden of despair.

Those raw, confusing, first few days dragged out into sweaty, twitchy,
weeks.
My skin crawled, my heart would race, then slow.
Floating listlessly in a swell of highs and lows, sleep became a
harbinger for dreams from a twisted universe.

I can tell you exactly how long it's been since I last revelled in your
company,
610 days, 20 hours, then some.

And not once did I cave, or crawl, beg, or break.

That's 610 days, 20 hours then some, since I last revelled in the taste of
    you on my lips,
since I held you in my fingers, since I breathed in your aroma,
since I had a drink.

Garry Cochrane

Wharfe

This is river water. Peat and mulch,
fish and cray and duck mites.

This is pool and swirl, tingle
and sting and never knowing

where the bottom is. Wharfe
from spring that flows to Leeds.

This river swim is brack and weeds,
bat and kingfisher-flash.

Head under, current-pull, eyes open,
ears full of water-speak.

River-flow, through fields,
run-off flood banks. Tonight

it is deep pond, flat surface, wide
and quiet. Mine.

Gill Connors

Prescription

Next day, driving my sad bones home
through sunshine and showers,
my heart laboured to birth compassion
for the empty seat beside me,
the blank page in the diary, the silent phone.

The analgesia as before:
one part Peter Gabriel's *I grieve*;
one part The Eagles *Get Over It*;
consume frequently, and walk, fast,
through woodland, and on windswept hills.

Hannah Stone

From my diary

I hate you, Dad, because you fixed my favourite doll.

*

From my diary, much later:

I love you, Dad, because you fixed my favourite doll.

Hans-Ulrich Heuser

Garlic

to plant garlic is to say I believe we will recover
to prise apart the papery gems, poke them
into cold clag and trust that despite the conditions
if we just hold our nerve, have faith, credit the earth
to know more than we do we will be rewarded
that November I water the cloves with my tears
return to Newcastle with Paisley dirt stubbornly stuck
under my nails sure enough come Spring the scapes appear
by summer they have twisted in on themselves,
grotesque swan necks kissing each other in a strangling embrace
flowering uselessly the bulbs go unharvested in my absence

Helen Rice

Restoration

Restoration is not always an option.
Life does not run by primogeniture
always producing a son and heir,
replacing deposed – even beheaded –
earlier eras of history. It just clambers
on from previous dethronement,
leaving us all as the Unrestored.

Isn't time always lost, not gained?
Even time travel cannot retrieve
a moment, as the traveller becomes
a fresh intrusion upon it, changing
that past anew. The past remains
another country, not the same one
as the strange place you entered.

For they have already done with all
those things they did so differently
there. To recover we too must differ.
To differ we must change. To change
we must break through time whilst
captive within it, crafting a new crown
not hollow but where life keeps court.

Helen Shay

Leaving holes

It took my dad three short weeks
from first chest pain to last breath.
His prognosis, always grim, a spell
come to blight us. A joking hole
left inside his Jeanie McSweeney,
their Girly Pearls, that's still there.
He fought back tears at our wedding.

Same age as my dad, my father-in-law
lived on in his pipe-smoking corner
of the retirement bungalow.
Anti-social, anti- most things,
he refused to come to our wedding.
He lived on and (I am not proud
to admit this) I resented his
humourless longevity. There,
I've said it out loud.

Parenting's a tricky thing to get right
and there's no blueprint. I just hope
I leave holes that don't hurt too much.

Hilary Robinson

The pain in my arse

started the day after I read my police report and examination. I got haemorrhoids five times. I got back pain later. I went to physio and got some exercises which aren't helping. Though the appointment was behind a curtain, and I couldn't really say the extra information *I think this might be body memories from getting paedoed when I was five.* The more I try the exercises, the more PTSD-y I feel. The more cranky I am.

I feel it all the way from my arse to my back now, I explain to my partner, which is a big step forward for me to say, because for the past few weeks there has just been the pain, and me trying to pretend: the pain isn't there; is something else; is this quiet kind of pain that needs to be looked after silently, and not disturbed or made to cry. My partner doesn't reply, leaves it for five minutes and asks *what are we doing at the weekend?* Which is more or less the response I expect from anyone and everyone else.

Holly Bars

Vital statistics

I am static,
Electric with nerves.
I am steeling myself
through a dark night.

I am a statistic,
one of the one in three
with the Big C,
my future determined
by a surgeon's verdict
to be delivered to me,
tomorrow, Tuesday.

My breast implant is sore
in its swelling seroma.
I slide my hand over its
alien size and shape.
It is immune to the touch, filleted in
to replace the cancered take-out,
a silicon mimic, laughably
ordered from a catalogue,
but can't be sent back.

My right vital statistic has inflated to a C,
a new bra necessitated,
I am now lop-sided in my cups,
but grateful I am here.
Can I reach the other side of five years
if I pluck the golden ticket of
no evidence of spread
in this life-lottery?

It's Tuesday.
I do not wake. I have not slept.
There is a blur of drive and park and walk,
then sitting rigid until my name is called.
Is the strange exchange
of pleasantries
a painful professional preface,
a delay of what-is-to-come?

I urge the surgeon on with my eyes,
but there is nothing in his face to tell
what finally he speaks in words
I find so hard to hear.
I have to check again,
but it seems the lymph nodes were, in fact,
clear
and I can live again,
ecstatic.

Jacqui Ambler

Social prescribing

I prescribe you a cabin in the Japanese mountains,
Some breathing space away from crowded society,
Where your only company will be the trees and wildlife.

I prescribe you distance away from any noise,
A place to calm your sense and that ruminating of yours,
Somewhere isolated from the touch of man.

Then when the time comes, I will prescribe social activity,
A healing balm for any isolated individual,
A shared hobby to reconnect with others when the time arrives.

Recover yourself from all that neighbourly noise.
Reset your life's baseline pulse and uproot somewhere new.
Rediscover it, all that genuinely matters to you.

Jaimes Lewis Moran

Frying pan – fire

Texas '83 off the main freeway – I nip behind the hedgerow and don my diversion outfit – the kilt, which proves a disaster! Eventually, one guy stops and tells us to get in. Driving an old Pontiac, curtains on the windows – pump-action shotgun hanging from the back sill, he spends the next hour lecturing us that *Judgement Day, Armageddon* – is fast approaching. He also tells us on that day – all blacks, commies, hippies and weirdoes – like me in my *skirt* – will be wiped from the face of the Earth! Our prophet is so intent on his sermon that he hasn't asked our destination, so, as soon as we come upon a Service Station we ask to be dropped there.

Making straight for the diner, Snowy goes for drinks – the hush is palpable – I head to the gents to change into jeans, I'm at a urinal when 6 cowboys enter forming a semi-circle behind me – standing, arms folded, silent. What to do? Zipping myself up, I turn and walk straight through them without making eye contact. Head low with one hand in front – I cleave a path between them. As we step outside and head towards the gas pumps, we know the next few moments will prove crucial. As luck would have it, a good old boy on his way back home to Bakersfield, pulls up and offers us a ride – to sunny California.

James Fernie

Worlds and wardrobes

As soon as she sees a tear in my tights
she reaches out for her haberdasher's kit
finest needle smallest eye
not-so-thin glasses
roughened fingers at a silken thread
the hole raring to take over
the entire length
Mum sutures the rectangle
making sure it doesn't run along my shin

Procrastinate hasn't been Mum's pattern
as a snap-on fastener comes loose
she prises out slack threads
steadies the shiny rim
in goes the threaded needle through the perforation
out it comes in it goes out it comes
till the base disc is firm enough
tich - the button's steely bauble settles snugly

Mum secures the eyelets of a bar
that dodders on a trouser waistband
double-checks the clasp
if it needs tightening
the hook rests taut in no time
upholding the trousers

Mum's always the first to spot a missing button
women's left and men's right
buttonholes grown too big for their partners
she tucks in the sloppy ones
both nestling well
natty fronts of savvy shirts
when a garter stitch sneaks down
from neck to midriff

Mum crochets it up singly
the jumper immaculate again

I never thought much of Mum's skills
it wasn't feminist enough
kept women tied to
thimbles, seam rippers, threaders,
collars, cuffs, hemlines
spooled in a spectrum of bobbins
off-whites and fawns to beiges and browns

It's taken me years to realise
Mum's life-long mending miscellanea
have sewn and resewn
our wardrobes and worlds together

Jaspreet Mander

Doing business upon the great waters

They that go down to the sea in ships, That do business in great waters –
Psalms

Dad flew search and rescue.
Days spent looking for bodies.

One time he walked around the chopper,
heard a squelch, looked down
at his foot through a bloated torso,
retched for hours

but still sky-owled the ocean for years
not so much for hope

but because once it had been him.

Jennifer A. McGowan

Healing power

Recently my husband and I were in a car accident and went to
      hospital.
Eventually we came home, although I came out before he did.
Carers and cardiac nurses were regular visitors, as well as the family.
Over the weeks we started to improve.
Visits to the hospital less frequent.
Every day we gained more strength, light gardening helped us a lot.
Regular exercise made us more mobile.
Youthful we will never be again, but we are not giving up, we'll keep on
      trying.

Joan Bosomworth

Return

And a heron flies near; none of that stepping
on grand-vizier legs, up it goes, angling its wings as if almost
Meccano; to reach deep, weeded water, breathing with fish.
We are haloed by autumn, freckled by rain.
The place pours in on us, a barrel of ripeness tipped
into our heads. Trees of rust, umber, bronze,
their leaves deep on our path. Then cloud lifts.
Sun blazes on slopes of massed ferns, those swathes
of chrome-yellow, burnt-orange, red; the whole aflame
above water that glows.
I go ahead, feasting on landscape,
wanting to capture all this. And turn
to see you, walking again, after so long away.
And the air replete with silence.

Josie Walsh

Green light

All quiet on Euston Road.
Mice skitter over the bare hostel bunks
and a cress seed, flushed from the last backpacker
to clean their teeth at the cupboard sink,
has lodged in the plughole
and gleaned enough lumens and grime
to raise its small green flag.

From a static sail of the unlit Moulin Rouge
a buddleia – *espèce envahissante* – cascades.
The plant's decay will trap grit
enough to feed saplings.

From a manhole cover
on Heathrow's disused Runway 1,
ragwort claws its way.

Purple loosestrife – drupe half-digested
by a Cedar waxwing – plumes
from a Times Square subway vent.

At the edge of the Darwin schoolyard
Where tarmac meets brick,
dandelions splay.

From hospital chimneys everywhere
fireweed waves, serene.

Sous les pavés la plage,
sous la plage la forêt.

Julia Deakin

47

Your hands

are frantic as landed fish today,
battling the seat belt, defiant car door.

At the café a trail of coffee hits the deck;
the sugar packet defeats your fingers.

That pointless biscuit makes for the exit,
the gulls applauding its parkour flourish.

The bullying café shakes the table.
Your custard tart crumbles, still in the foil,

slathers over your shirt.
I recover the bit that is still good.

There, good as new. Ten second rule! Not five,
stretching time the only way we can.

Julie Griffiths

Seasons

Spring. Eliot said April was the cruellest month. Memory, like dew, wept all over the lawn, sturdy daffodils were chastened by showers; by May all the poppies had been defrocked. Weeds were sprouting, and the house: the house hadn't had a chance to air after the endless days of the wood burner, its soot talcuming places you could hardly imagine!

Now summer, everyone longs for summer and Shakespeare takes some responsibility for that. The sun got hot in July. The curtains faded protecting the Afghan carpets that had miraculously held on to their azure gardens and magenta flowers for years, and she didn't really have a nice hat to wear after losing the straw one she bought in Naples when Dennis was alive.

Autumn could be wet, outside of the famed mists, and heaven knows Keats had a lot to answer for; it was often drizzly, the pavement coated with an inky shine that made her skate to the shop in her rubber-soled boots. It could also be a bit windy, enough to dry the sheets, but also enough to damage the sapling she'd planted in spring.

Now, most definitely in the winter of her life, as Dennis had said from the frozen sheets of his hospital bed, she did tend to mither a bit about things: burst pipes and the back bedroom walls decorated with mildew. But Rossetti was right – winter was full of secrets – she thought as the snowflakes flung themselves at her open mouth.

Kay Boardman

The Continuing Life Of Janet's Foss

Ramshackle stone barn, ram skull sentry,
path snakes by serpent-scale money-trees,
wood-sorrel, ramson scent, sycamore
roots ooze with sludge water in the copse

like blood from warm corpses till the force
of gravity drops white tangled locks
lank about the shy faerie face, life
from death reclaimed, rams the hollow full,

our amphitheatre brimming with Herb
Robert, spleenwort tang, hart's-tongue fern, moss,
limestone tufa dressed with wall-rue tufts,
our foss floats lifeless in cool clear pools.

Keith Fenton

Tomb raider

I get it. I'm a tomb raider. It's in my family. My greatest ancestor was one and my greatest mission is Rome and Greece. Athens, the city of Rome, Venice. I'm Italian and Greek, so I like to be around them. Italy with its Colosseum, and the temples of the Roman gods. I love them all and their mythologies.

My favourite is the one about King Midas' golden touch. I need to recover some of all this and, yes, sell it. My family needs to do this. But I know that if I get caught, I will be arrested. What I do is illegal. But it's worth it. The thrill is amazing.

Brodie

Dig, dig, dig

Dig, dig, dig, I absolutely love *digging*.

I love the mystery of unlocking the secrets of our past, I love the thrill of the jackhammer ringing its precious soothing bells echoing across the lands of our archaeology site, I love the sensation of opening a never-opened-before door hiding a world of opportunity, I love, I love, I - Sorry, as you can probably tell, **I love digging**, but today is where my love, my passion could only reach so high.

You're probably wondering what the hell I'm going on about but today, whilst doing my regular digging (**I LOVE DIGGING**) there was an unusual shriek, reverberating its lust for freedom through the site. My curiosity shrunk as my excitement diminished, all meshing into - not the thrill of the mystery, but the fear of the unknown. However, it was my job to dig up what hasn't yet been seen, my duty to recover the past.

And so, as I traversed through the desert of gusts, I saw the hole. I didn't see where it led to. I didn't know who had dug it. I had no idea at all. Oh boy, I really wish I'd just stayed at home today...

Cristiano

Pieces by pupils from Leeds East Academy

From war

Dear Diary,

You would never believe what I did like eighty years ago that I am still processing and recovering from, because it was terrifying.

I fought in World War Two with my two best friends. All of us was terrified because we were only seventeen years old. I wasn't even an adult, yet my two friends were eighteen years old. However, back to the point.

On the way to the battleground, me and my friends were talking to each other about our family and what we would do if we survived this. John said *Try and get a normal job and spend most of my time with my family.* Then Max said *I would probably look after my family and friends.* I told them I didn't know.

Surprisingly it only took like an hour to get there on a boat. Me and my friends got on the battleground. We did have to split up for a bit sadly. All I was hearing was shooting, planes, tanks and screams. By the end of the day I was covered in mud.

After ducking in the trenches, I finally met up with my friend. I asked Max where John was. He said he got shot. I started to cry my eyes out, but then behind me there was soldier that was about to shoot me. My friend Max sacrificed himself so he was shot and I caught him and he was laying dying in my arms. It was so hard to watch. I never witnessed anything like this before.

I still miss them both today. I feel so guilty, like it was my fault that Max died because he sacrificed himself for me. I feel responsible, because if it wasn't for them both, I wouldn't be here to tell you my story now.

This whole experience haunts me forever and ever, probably till I die. I just wish they were still here so they can do the stuff they said they would do if they survived this bloody war. Why did this war even start? I am done talking about it today. Bye.

Lacey

She

In the hushed even-fall and twilight hours, as the tenebrous cumulonimbus converges on, the echo of frustration around; as the heavenly body witnesses my wailing, my heart, the last ember of a spent candle flickers in the dark. When the cage of misfortune trapezes me helpless, her arms are a shielding sanctuary from the pernicious world. As Time drifts like a cloud in the gloomy vast sky, I feel lost.

But she is my guardian angel, her guidance a tapestry of altruistic support and love, her presence an unfound treasure. She invests herself, her time, her dreams, her hopes. Being a mother isn't easy, she faces frequent pain yet always gives a welcoming embrace and a warm smile.

Her sacrifices are nothing but a god's gift which always supports and helps my wellbeing. Thanking her would never be enough because she has always been a compass that leads me to the right path. When no one helps me get out of certain nightmares, she changes my gloomy life into a bright heaven.

Meghnaa

Life of a timekeeper

Karl sighed, softly climbing the pretty-much endless ladder which would probably kill you if you missed a step.

He eventually made it to the top. Hoisting himself up, he took a breath of relief and looked at the large pockets, each carrying a different world within. Some were good, some were bad, but to poor Karl they were his worst nightmare.

He set his bag down. Running a hand through his fluffy brown hair, he sat cross legged, grabbing his bag and pulling it towards him. Unzipping it, he pulled out a small tub of cashews. It may be a strange craving to you, but it's Karl's favourite snack guaranteed.

As he ate, he felt a clawed hand grab his hood and drag him backward. In a flight or fight reaction, he shot the creature dead, kicking it back into its world, then made sure to zip the pocket up. It was going to be a long day for Karl.

Robyn

Eden

I would call her Eden but honestly, she's even more beautiful than anyone could ever imagine. Words cannot capture the essence of her picturesque landscapes covered by towering mountain ranges that we stand on. However, when we do refer to her, we call her our motherland.

That's why we are called the Children of the Sun. It's because we are the closest people to the brightest thing in our solar system, the thing that lights up our lives and makes the worst situation feel even slightly better. The warmth of its rays calms me and I aspire every day to be that thing in someone else's life.

But humans destroy everything that they encounter, so what was once a place we called heaven became a monstrosity filled with trauma that was covered by the mountains, trapped, just waiting to come out. Hundreds of thousands died but our mountains masked the truth. What my people thought were the forgiving rays of the sun shining were the merciless chemical bombs that, instead of warming us, just burned our hands and faces.

But we survived and we became stronger. The stepping stones of history have shaped us and revealed this to be true. Even when the world turned its back or left us to become lost in the history of humanity and its evil doings, we still rose up and managed to keep our name, keep our dignity. Though the world has spat in our face and closed its eyes, even stolen our home away from us, we have still managed to keep our culture.

So, though I might have to tick the box of Iraqi when something asks me what country I come from, in my heart I will always be Kurdish.

Zhiri

It was the best of times, it was the worst of times

Have we ever fully recovered from the Covid years?
Some still suffer with long term symptoms
Although physically, most of us survived
Mentally it is a different story

We followed the rules set by scientists and the government
Craving reassurance that in doing so all would be well
Stoically accepted vaccines, donned masks and stayed in our bubbles
Applauding the NHS for carrying on regardless

Some of us fared better than others
Those with gardens had extra space for outdoor play
Those with the resources could home school their children
Meanwhile anxiety, depression and domestic violence increased
        behind closed doors

We looked forward to a decrease in the spread of the virus
So everything could return to what was before
To be able to return to school or the workplace
To meet up again with our friends and family

We made grand plans for holidays and shopping sprees
To meet people face-to-face instead of online
To celebrate birthday parties and weddings together
Or go down the pub or eat in a restaurant

Had we lost the knack of socialising and working together?
Were we still grieving our loved ones lost too early?
Did we still put our trust in those who we thought would protect us?
Was it the best of times or the worst of times?

Linda Casper

Found

the body has been recovered
and something in my life goes missing

no longer do I fill the emptiness
with news reports
drip feeding me tittle-tattle
my curiosity no longer hungers
for more detail

shouldn't I have known
it's not a game, not an Agatha Christie
it involves a real person, real people

the body has been recovered
nobody in the vicinity gets over this

I think I've lost my way

Linda Marshall

Suboptimal

Somehow the situation was *suboptimal*. *Sub* in relation to *mountain peak* is not normally unusual, after all, statistically speaking, very few people live *super* a mountain peak. But my *sub* was different.

I had just climbed the Rastkogel at an altitude of 2,762 meters when a bullet from Pelikan's rifle grazed my calf.

Asshole! I shouted indignantly as my left leg gave way and my heavy hiking backpack accelerated my fall. Unfortunately, I did not fall forward onto the slope, but sideways down a rock. Three meters below the rock, I landed relatively softly on my backpack. Unfortunately, I did not come to rest, but instead slid uncontrollably down the scree field. Instinctively, I grabbed for large stones, but they were not heavy enough and slid down the slope with me.

Suddenly, nothing under my hands. Another fall. *Shit*, I thought eloquently. That's what people think when they're about to fall from a 2,000-meter-high mountain.

But the fall was only another 2 meters. Smack, ouch, rolling stones again, standstill. Finally.

Alive. Breathing. Looking around.

I was lying on a rocky outcrop. Above me the silhouette of the summit cross against the sun. Below me a fall of at least 300 meters. Suboptimal.

A scream echoed through the valley. The stones around me were shaking. I wished the person up there would be calm. Then they were. For a long time nothing happened. I lay there and breathed, recovered.

Finally, the sound of rotor blades.

Linn Schiffmann

The trouble with over-used metaphors

It was never the contrived metaphor of a road.
That would suggest we could reach the end,
and a recovery of sorts.
Instead, you and I tread a hostile landscape,
sometimes together, sometimes alone.
I never know when our paths will converge,
when they might veer sharply away from each other
and we both have to go it alone
for a while.

I don't see all of the landscape you are made to walk
in solitude,
but I imagine you scrambling over rocks,
wading through muddied water,
dodging rock falls,
skidding down scree on steep slopes.
You acquire cuts and grazes along the way,
I see blood and mud seep through your clothes,
watch purple heather bloom on vulnerable skin,
wish I could soothe it away as I once did,
with cool springwater, words blown on the wind,
love.

But now I am useless, can only
watch and wait until our paths converge again,
walk the next part with you, scale mountains,
plough the expanse of empty fields,
let my hair and voice loose on summits
to scream the unfairness and cruelty of it all,
hold your trembling hands,
try to see your terrified face in the dark,
find a more fitting metaphor.

Lisa Falshaw

Ode to a ghost

In the dusty corners of the old chapel, where sunlight danced through new stained-glass windows, a ghostly figure hovered.

For as long as anyone could remember, Harold Greenbottom's ghostly presence had been accompanied by a massive aura of fear. A mere mention of his name would send a shiver down the spine.

But not anymore.

Harold found himself struggling to maintain his reputation. His moans had lost their chill, his apparitions had become as ethereal as a wisp of smoke, and his ability to make objects levitate had degraded to a mere wobble. It was as if the very essence of his haunting powers had gone, people had grown accustomed to his antics, barely flinching when a microphone trembled on its stand or a cold breeze brushed past them unannounced.

The chapel had changed much since his time. The once solemn sanctuary had been transformed into a bustling arts centre, a place where music echoed off the vaulted ceilings and children's giggles filled the once hushed air now charged with the energy of creation, leaving little room for the chilling whispers of the dead.

Harold knew he had to do something. It wasn't just his pride at stake. If word got out that he couldn't even spook a cat, the ghost hunters might come knocking, armed with their gadgets and exorcism rituals they might send him over to the other side. He had to recover his title as the chapel's most feared resident before it was too late...

Liz Dawson

Coping

Today we walked the dogs.
I noticed how thin you've got, how you flinched
when Oscar pulled on his lead.
I said, *I think it's a bad back, that it might go away
after a few days rest* and you nod.

We sit in your too-neat lounge, drinking tea;
you mention you're going for another blood transfusion
at Bexley Wing and I want to shout, *let's gallop across fields,
pretend we're event riders at Bramham, let's jump off
the iron bridge over the river, let's eat chocolate till we're sick,
steal daffodils from the park.*

Instead, we talk about how you think your house
needs a lick of paint, how the bathroom is calling
for a good spring clean, how the clock in the kitchen
has stopped.

Liz McPherson

Walking on new legs

I left this country whole, came back diminished,
though the nerves insisted that was wrong,
sparking and firing after the surgeon finished,
fizzing along the pathways that were gone.
I've dreamt of walking, just as you dream of flying –
weightlessness, that unexpected lift,
and then the impossible: without even trying,
surging through space – sleep's temporary gift.
Diminished: that's not the word for what became
of me. You think you understand my war?
Well-meaning friends insist I'm still the same.
The truest know, if anything, I'm more.
    You still dream of soaring like a hawk
    but this is real. Come. Watch me walk.

Lydia Kennaway

Tree

An open lump
On no active pathway,
Few will pass by,
A wasted witness
Lying keeled over,
Blackened by fire.
Silken smoothness withstanding,
Bare, to be done unto.
Scrubbed-up ends, flame-shrunken cells
Sap withdrawn
Deadness, dead, dead.

A heart with chopped-off open veins and arteries
Hollow, black-rimmed,
Feeding nothing,
Prolonging no life,
Maintaining no communing spirit,
Stopped.

Stopped, chopped, amputated.
Once penetrating earth,
Once linked in the fruitful cycle
Of growth and burgeoning,
Green, brown, fall,
Change to inner secret life,
Waiting, preparation, growing
For another year
To produce, to exult in
Fertility.

Then with stark brutality
Uplifted, torn, stricken
By wind and power all unknow
To be laid aside
Prey to forces of decay
Wildness and passion tamed,
Waiting, but passive now,
Waiting for the long absorption into earth
To be, free and wholly given.
A tree.

Powerless now, the tree lies
Still, offering to restless human hearts
The questions, challenges of life
And meaning of our earthly trail.
This wounded mass,
This naked history portraying
Rings of endurance,
Through battling storms
And still reflection,
Points us to a larger span
Of conversation:
As armies, nations, wearily repeat
The human struggle,
Confrontation, needing to be right,
A wounded trunk weeps,
And bids us listen
To quiet echoes of hope.

Madeleine Andrews

From the beach

The worn brick nestles in the wooden surround, settled in sand. One box frame contains articles past reclaiming – only one sock, a flattened can, snapped plastic pieces, frayed cables, broken glass. Bits of detritus recovered to recycle and clean up the environment but framed like this, they create a story, a challenge.

Trapped in time, framed – caught in the act of becoming meaningful because placed in a different setting. How do I see? Do I see the possible, the what if...? What is rubbish? What is worn out and discarded but can take on new meaning? Juxtaposition, context, proximity – all words with an 'x' that marks the unknown potential inherent in these leftovers.

As we recover the discarded, we uncover potential and open our eyes and minds to look more deeply, more creatively. When we immerse ourselves in wave-washed debris and give ourselves permission to play, we slow down. We see from a different angle which in turn brings a different focus. Worn driftwood looks ancient but may only be as old as immersion in a rough sea through a few tides. Stripped bare and tumbled smooth, it asks to be touched.

Memories of holidays on the beach as children, building castles, making shapes in the sand, playing with the sea. A breathing space in which to re-set the body's clock.

Madeleine Wuidart

Equanimity restored

Life can damage body and soul
Destroying, ravaging, exhausting
A tsunami of loss and pain
Acute, overwhelming, ceaseless
An agony to be endured
Even as the roots are severed
Hurt remains inextricably entwined
Clinging to an unwilling host
A reminder of sorrow and regret
Time ebbs and flows
Memories fade, but a spark, they ignite
As sharp and destructive as ever
Eventually equanimity is restored
And it's a slow climb to recovery.

Mally Harvey

Jack-in-the-pulpit

Almost as soon as I could walk,
I was devotional; I toddled
my secret pilgrimage down the driveway,
squatted on unboned haunches,
and stroked with reverence
the trumpet lilies growing there.

Raindrops slid down arum throats,
flicked splashes on silken leaves,
furled petals cool to touch,
even in the furnace of the day.
I glided baby fingers on turgid stamens,
whorls gilded argentine for life.

I don't know why, but I recover
the memory many years later,
when the rivers turn to blood.
We were unprotected that day,
but not in the way I thought.
I thought we were intentional:

I was the paradise setting,
a tropical waterfall in moonshine,
closed around a preacher in the night.
I was so sure that tiny, pink spiders
could hold on; that no ambrosial,
funeral flower, could ever let you go.

Mandy Schiffrin

Buoys will be buoys

The refuse dump on the small island is cleverly sited in a natural fold of the coast. No vehicles, except perhaps a tractor, can get anywhere near it.

But whenever I stay on this island, I always walk to the dump to see what's on offer. Mangled children's trikes, planks of wood, moth-eaten carpet fragments, tyres, broken pots and pans.

This time I spotted a huge, pink, netted fishing buoy, which used to be used for any creels and with glass fishing floats. It was possibly fourteen inches in diameter, intact and ensconced by its original diamond-shaped 'net' of thin rope. A hefty hawser was attached to the top. I decided that the buoy would look great in my back garden 250 miles away.

Picking up the buoy I was astounded by its weight. So how to carry it to the bunkhouse a mile away, and then onto the ferry to the mainland where my car was parked?

On the other side of the dump, I found a wooden pole about three feet long, and attached it to the buoy's hawser. I then used the pole to heave the buoy onto the ground and, negotiating rivulets, marsh and rocks, dragged it along to the road.

It was much easier to roll the buoy along the tarmac. I soon met an islander who was heading for the beach. *Hello!* she said, *You're taking your buoy for a walk!*

I grinned. She was taking her boy for a walk.

Marg Greenwood

Camp fire dreams

Flames weave and dance as the fire burns bright.
Firefly sparks cast away into the dark.
Is that to be our fate?
The human race incandescent but for a moment?

Images of the future writhe within the flames:

A world ravaged by war.
The lust for power ending only in annihilation.
Cities?
Destroyed.
People?
Wiped out.
No surviving the bombing, the radiation, the tragedy.

Too wise for that, I hear?
But not wise enough.
Not wise enough to heed the warnings,
The rising temperatures,
The melting ice,
The droughts and the floods.

Not wise enough to look ahead
Until too late
And we create a world in which we cannot survive.

Ah! Look there!
We did listen!
We're smart.
We're inventive.
We've ransacked the planet to feed our desires.
It can support us no more
And we are gone.

But the flames dance on.

The gentle rain and the crashing waves
Smooth away the scars of our passage.
Once proud buildings that we saw
As a testament to progress
Are being reclaimed,
Unable to withstand Earth's natural forces.
Though humanity is gone,
Life thrives.
Plants and trees take back the cities.
Insects adapt.
New life evolves.

And once again
A blue and white jewel of a planet
Sparkles in the velvet blackness of space.

Margaret Bending

In the Cairngorms

I see what storms did to trees last week,
up close, as if I have suffered from the damage.
Life is about trip hazards once again:
deadfall, the corpses of hazels lying there
waiting to be cut up and taken away.
Other trees have died without falling,
recumbent, propped up by old friends,
like those who propped me up.
Many paths are cordoned off by tape
as if this is a murder scene to investigate
by the Forestry Commission. Utter carnage.
Folk I see out walking look like they had grieved each loss.

I'm in recovery too, like the trees storms left behind.
A friend was lifted from the earth,
a man who seemed to wear life lightly,
even when things didn't go his way.
I still feel anger at his final text:
Let's catch up when all this is over.
We never did and I try not to hold it against him.
But it's good to feel anger when you grieve.
It stops the numbness setting in, so you can hear
the remaining trees trying to tell you something.
And the rich yellow gorse along the roads,
how it shines on, even when the sun can't find you.

Mark Connors

Recovered from memory

Recovery is such a useful word. It can be a noun – the recovery of someone or something and a verb– to recover. And it's a very positive word. Being an optimist, I imagine that whatever it is that has been recovered is positive and not negative, like happy days, picnics and friendship, recovered from memory.

And of course there is personal recovery from some unwelcome state of being. Here I think of my mother and her many recoveries. At 21 she recovered from the flu in the 1918 flu epidemic, while her beloved sister Dorothy died. She had lost her mother as a child and endured a dominating father. When she married at 26, she foresaw a happy future and gave birth to twins a year later. However, her husband was violent and neglectful, a frustrated intellectual, more interested in philosophy and music than family. But with the help of her half-brother, she was able to get away from him and build a new life for herself and the twins, eventually supporting the family by running a Post Office.

Throughout her life she depended on good friendships – like Lizzie, her childhood friend, Emily who worked with her at the Post Office, and in later life a friend who shared her intellectual interests, known always as Miss Franklin. Looking back, I credit her recovery to these intellectual interests and her ability to sustain such loyal friendships. And I admire her courage to survive the hardships she suffered – and still to recover.

Mary Cooper (Senior)

A-rhythm

When he found the surgeon-man
amongst the lanes of asbestos-
substitute and paint-splashed glass,
he was sitting on a swivel-stool,
between two towers of mock Swedish
office furniture, humming loudly,
a tune from the 90's, drumming
faster as the song built to a banger.

He handed the surgeon-man the form
with the three pastel carbon sheets
and the one question printed
at the top, demanding a description
of *the patient's heart, in terms of size,*
rhythm, and a simple prognosis.

Looking out from on high, across
the town in freefall, over the columns
of red-brick rooms, fat-packed pantries,
hearing only the shenanigans of the
surgeon-man's pen on the NHS paper,
as he wrote: *Patient's heart is fat. It taps*
like a mad spaniel on pitch black ice.
He is sliding this way and that, towards
the busy motorway.

Matt Nicholson

Saturday night and Sunday morning

1982 A Terraced House in Leeds

Make the ringing stop. Oh my head
Who's phoning at this time on a Sunday?
It'll be Jane, checking to see we got home alright
Have you still got your clothes on?
I couldn't manage the buttons last night, but I did get my shoes off
What's this wine doing here?
You said you wanted another drink when we got in, so we brought it to
bed
Take it away, just the smell
Why do we do it. Every Saturday night we meet at 7.30pm in the
Viaduct. Then it's round to the Peel, before ending up at Charlie's till
2am
Because all our friends do it
I'm not moving today, I can't
Yes, you are, you know we all meet up at 12 in the Viaduct to compare
notes from last night
Have we got any money left?
Don't know till I find my trousers
When the pub shuts at 2pm we'll come straight home. Don't accept any
invites to carry on drinking at somebody's house in the afternoon
Make some coffee while I get a quick shower
I'll dial 1471 and check who was calling
Can we afford a taxi? I can't walk to the bus
We'll have to stop at a Cash Machine
I think we should stay in tonight; we need to recover for work
tomorrow
I think we should, but I don't suppose we will. We never do.

Michael Hassell

Bananas

When you eat a banana you probably don't give it a second's thought. I however, know that bananas helped me in my recovery from depression. To me depression is a form of temporary insanity, because what sane person would see suicide as the only way out of their problems? I was in such a dark place in my head that I planned my own death. I visited several chemists and purchased the maximum number of paracetamol that was allowed. I spent all the money I had on the tablets and an enormous chocolate cake, which was weird because by this time I was eating very, very little. It was in some way my idea of my final meal. It was my one glimmer of triumph in my final hours, I would eat my cake, take the tablets, go to sleep and not wake up.

I was absolutely devastated to wake up in hospital to the realisation that I couldn't even succeed in ending my life. I was so ill I spent 3 months in the mental health ward of my local hospital. I would go to the dining room if I was escorted there by a member of staff but wouldn't eat anything. The staff slowly got me to eat again with bananas. My first meal was half a banana, eventually I could manage to eat a whole banana. I smile now at the sight of a banana and still turn to bananas as a comfort food.

Mick Robinson

Past and present

The foundations of early life broken, almost derelict.
The best upbringing you could ever dream of.

The past numb, cold and hazy, the future almost unimaginable.
A childhood remembered with love and fondness, excited for new
    adventures.

Some survived, some thrived, all still alive.

Regaining strength and possession of self. Feeling proud of who they
    are!

Recovered (some still a work in progress).

Nancy Elwell

Winter, remember

Winter, remember, is all underground,
winter's thoughts run deep,
thinking but keeping its thoughts to itself
deep in its wintry sleep.
The late rose that burns on a winter's day
ignites the fuse of spring,
mistletoe, cherry and jasmine catch fire,
flames dance, flowers sing.

Neil Rathmell

Pillow talk

Can't sleep again?
How did you —?
Know? Love. Feels like I'm spooning a statue.
...
Bit tense, yeah?
I'm sorry.
Nah, don't be.
...I wish it were easier.
Yeah.
It should be easy. Ridiculous that it still... affects me like it does. It
*   was years ago.*
Yeah. But brains hold onto things, don't they?
Well, I wish they would hold onto more useful things.
Me too. Maybe I wouldn't've flopped all my geography tests. Hey.
*   Look at me?*
...
How long've we been together? Sleeping next to each other like this?
Five years, seven months, two weeks. Approximately.
And in all that time, have I ever let anything bad happen to you?
No. Of course not.
Yeah, 'course not! Anyone comes in here after you, they're gonna
*   have to get through me.*
I know. I know. That's what makes it so frustrating. I'm the safest I've
*   ever been, and still...*
Yeah. Yeah, I know, love.
...
How many days in five years, seven months, two weeks?
Two thousand and fifty-two. Not accounting for leap years.
So that's over two thousand nights between you and what happened.
Yes... Yes, I suppose it is.
C'mere. Let's try for one more. Maybe you'll believe me after the next
*   thousand, eh?*

I want to believe you now!
I know. But it's alright that you don't.
...
I'll wear you down eventually, love. Promise.

Newton Albrecht

One step at a time

Stumble, fall, get up, this is how we learn as infants to walk. If we didn't get up and try again, we would never learn the next step. I didn't think this and relate it to my recovery until I did fall... Just stepping without thinking, foot catching, falling forward. My face got the full force and between me and the lamp post my soft pliable skin had come off worse. I looked in the mirror, what a mess! My skin mottled black and red, my matted unwashed hair hung around my shoulders, my clothes from another life were now dirty and in need of a wash. I looked like I had been in a fight. How could I now get on the bus and go to my meeting? I had already experienced the cold loneliness of nobody wanting to sit next to me... no, it was impossible, I couldn't go.

Stumble, fall, get up... one foot in front of the other. I was there, people spoke to me, everyone was concerned and someone sat next to me. I remembered, I had changed my clothes, I had washed.

I smiled – a tiny part of me glowed, a warm feeling of confidence filling my consciousness. As I stood up to leave, my head felt heavy, and I stumbled.

Stumble, hold on, step forward. As I got my balance, I realised this is life, I am a survivor. One step at a time, moving slowly, I am recovering.

Nicki Powell

Ripley Wood

I sip new water, crave the stilling and sharpening of my senses,
kind sunlight, fluttering birds, hushed bushes,
holding trees, papery leaves,
my canopy from function to freedom.

Nicola Good

A version of therapy

Recovery takes many forms. Sometimes it's a matter
of steady hands and predictable sleep, sometimes it's
cold tiles behind a locked door, but always the losses
outweigh the gains. On one side of the scales, I pile
pills, phone numbers, acronyms, and breathing
exercises; on the other, I place memory, forgetting,
blunt nails, and broken glass. I adopt a balanced diet
of water and dust, but my gut's full of rocks, and each
morning I'm heavier than the night before. I adopt a
stray dog, but he's a coyote, or a tsunami, or a
recurring nightmare of being buried alive. I adopt an
air of calm, but that's someone else, and I retreat to
my panic room, reciting my superstitious litany of safe
words. Yet, I have recovered my bloated body from the
pond in the park, and I have recovered the chairs and
sofa to hide the stains. Recovery is a matter of steady
sleep and predictable hands. Sometimes it's just a
matter of filling in forms and waiting.

Oz Hardwick

Anastrozole

She's reached halfway; two and a half years to go of this miracle drug. The packet says; *take one per day until May 2027*. She wonders what she'll be when she reaches the other side. The paper insert is clear. She'll be old, with fading bones, a crone. Nodal osteoarthritis means wearing glamorous gloves to bed but it's okay. *A temporary problem* she tells herself *You're still alive. Don't moan. You can do this*. Remembers her old dad wearing his rupture truss like a gunslinger. How he listened to the news all night. Couldn't cope with day.

She knows lying awake is inevitable. Distracts herself with Audible, feeding into earbuds until morning; Josephine Tey detective stories with *bright young things* who speak their minds, Bertie Wooster, Crompton's *Just William* – the way books in the nineteen twenties and thirties lied. How they had food and titles and empire; bravura in the face of fascism. How they'd done the war to end all wars. The flu to end all flu's. Threw stones at the Black Shirts in Bristol.   Until it came back.

But this isn't war, she tells herself. Not yet. Enjoy life! The climate cataclysm isn't quite here. Grow up. You're just one more woman not wanting nature to win.

Pen Kease

M62. Junction 27.

I left late. Darkness already creeping
into the chill February day.
But I got a shift on, felt the warmth
of you all waiting grow steadily
with every fog-thickened mile.

I was so close. Two junctions.
Then the noise
of something snapping,
unratcheting inside the engine.
Loss of power. Just enough
to scrape onto the shoulder –

narrow here, as the carriageway
bridged over other roads.
Behind the barrier, only the thinnest strip
of scrub, concrete-rooted.
I balanced myself
between the fear of falling
or of being hit by a truck,
rattling round the bend, oblivious.

Except one. A transit.
He saw me with enough time to slow,
to stare and see me through the bloom of fog.
My heart slowed too,
limbic system playing catch-up.
I remembered that woman,
the pregnant one in '88.

He was gone, but the prickle
and dry mouth remained.
I shrank back further,
tried not to feel the abrupt space

behind me. Tried not to let
the cold settle too deep inside me.

I waited for the orange lights
of the flat-bed, flashing
recovery round the junction.
Overlaid inside my mind
with flashing blue and red.

Penny Blackburn

You won't recover from this!

Tell us why you think you're the best candidate for the job.

It's been my dream ever since I was a child. I've studied it at University for three years and I was awarded a First. Before that I did it for 2 years at A level and got an A star. I know the competition is fierce out there, but please, please, please if you give me a chance I won't disappoint you. It's what I was put on this earth to do!

I'm sorry, but I don't think you're what we are looking for.

Why not?

You're overqualified and you won't stay if something better comes along.

How can you possibly be overqualified for training to be a barrister?

I agree, but you can be overqualified to train to be a barista.

Oh shit, I've spent a fortune getting here, took a day off work, unpaid and bought this fancy suit.

You've learnt the hard way, son. Spelling matters.

Pete Tidy

Great Recovery

I pulled a muscle, long tale short. Shooting pain in my calf. I felt the muscle tear. I'm limping about.

Don't worry, I'll be alright.

I saw the doctor. It looks worse than it is. Even rode my bike briefly and hiked around Victoria Lake.

Then it happened all quite suddenly. The pain travelled like flu through my leg. It swelled up - a red balloon.

I'm lying there in hospital looking up at the ceiling. Feeling terrified. Hobbling to the bathroom. Heart racing, not knowing whether I'm dying or living. Should I write a will?

A shot cheers me prior to vascular surgery. Terrifying blood tests. Fears of infection. Lying there in layers of vulnerability. Nurses Doctors Porters and Health Workers. All of life is lived through a Canula.

I plead with them not to discharge me too early.

OK they say, but don't look now as a stent is fitted painfully into my vein. Balloon Angioplasty gets that vein open again.

My friends call, hospital visiting, bringing me grapes!

Nine years later I'm still here.

Thanks to the Vascular Team at the Leeds General Infirmary!

Peter McDonagh

Look and listen

The woods are awake.
The trees are stirring.
It feels different today,
walking through them.

I sense subtle movements invisible to the eye,
an intangible magic hangs in the air
Fresh life hums through bare bones.

I stand
still.
I watch.
And I listen.
Their pulsing presence radiates to my beating heart.
This rhythm of life connects us in a shared sacred moment.

Showers of white blackthorn blossom
shimmer softly amidst stark silhouettes of dark bark and green moss.
A confetti explosion of early spring joy.

Some trees speak.
If I'm slow and steady enough, I hear them.

The tall beech trunks divided in two,
tell me about balance.
The presence of two halves,
One is no greater than the other.
Hold the whole in your awareness.
Allow it all.

A cheerful, cheeky, mystery tree
stands separately. Happily alone,
near ancient hedgerows. Proudly independent,
near a companionable gathering of friends.
It shows me how to stand in the space I need.
Be you. You're enough as you are.
Enjoying company and connections.

Two majestic scarred sisters, stand tall.
They remind me how time passes,
that challenges change,
storms come and go.

Their strength and a full, long life lived is clear to see.
It comforts me.
Through the woods I will wander, never alone.

Rachel Clark-Wilson

I just wish Howard would do one

Several times a week I recover from dementia
and if you think that seems improbable, think again:
recovery's a wayward dream for Lewy body patients
but for me, watching you slowly fade into fantasy,
recovery, by which I mean the need to restore
myself, is a must after sharing your parallel universe
where Howard is trying to steal our farmhouse,
make us bankrupt, take everything – including me
and the solicitors are doing nothing about it and you
won't eat your lunch because you just had lunch
with Amie, Angus and me at the meeting with Howard
and I say *no, we had to leave before lunch was served,
remember, Amie had to get to work, so please
eat your lunch and you say if I eat this do I get to keep
the farmhouse* so I nod, watch you fork in a mouthful
while talking to Joan-Who's-Become-Howard across
the table and Joan answers from her own broken reality
so nothing here makes sense and if it wasn't so totally
sad it might almost be funny so after two hours
I come home, sit in the garden with a cup of Rooibos.
I'm on my third stint in recovery this week.

Rachel Davies

One step

Slowly, Slowly
They tell me
As I move along the solid
Yet strangely swaying floor.

Shift weight;
Slowly, slowly,
Lift leg;
Slowly, slowly

The goal is precision,
In a simple movement.
Finally;
Through sheer determination
And pleading,
A miracle happens...

One Step!

Rachel Flint

Feeling better / Sich besser fühlen

Im Regen gehen
mit 125 €
in der Tasche
& gleich Kuchen
kaufen ist das
nicht herrlich!

> Walking in the rain
> with €125
> in the pocket
> & soon to buy
> cake isn't that
> wonderful!

Im Garten
auf der Bank sitzen
in der Sonne
die Wolken ziehen
über mich hinweg
und ich
ziehe mit

> In the Garden
> sitting on the bench
> in the sun
> clouds are passing
> over me
> and I pass
> with them

Ralf Thenior

In Calverley Street

Time has spared the retired School Board building,
that stirs a memory in one passing.
We were children and lay on rush-green mats,
listening as Miss taught us to relax.
With steady beat she incanted a rhyme,
and bid us follow while keeping in time.
Halting and starting, the rhyme made its rounds
with awkward stops and caught-in-the-throat sounds.
Miss guided us like our second mother,
coaxing forth voices that lay undiscovered.
Tony she saw approach the Slow-Tongued Boy,
intrigued by his turnout, school shirt and tie.
Posh, the word Tony fought to deliver,
shot past his lips in a shower of spittle.
The other smiled, as hesitation waned,
and with lagging tongue told Tony his name.
They paired up like one divided by two.
Tony gave him a poke: *You're alright, you.*
As building and memory passed from view,
I told my lost friend he was alright too.

Robert Hill

The skid

Midnight
and this snake of country road
is a gift
for wannabe Formula One posers.
    They screech
left,
    right,
        abandon stomach to brow.
I steer into flashes of headlights
    a race of overtakes
wipers wiped I spin
    360

Spotify plays my thudding heart.

    Instinct dictates
I climb through the gears
    follow the moon's spectral beam
keep to the left of double whites
    and ask
who or what cleared the game board?

Sandra Burnett

...And breathe

One day, another day, not today
As I was churning and turning hue
Darker than usual, rather blue
My sister, kindly, did say
Try not to stress and to seethe
Please, just remember to breathe

Please sister, please, just breathe
In and out, in and out
That's what it's all about
In and out, in and out
Sister, you can, just breathe
In and out, in and out

Now, breathe with me sister
...and breathe

Sarah Rooke

Fairy tales of the mind

She wanted herself back.
The girl who could look in the mirror and smile without it being a lie
Without picking up on each fault and flaw
Until all she could see was a treasure map of things to fix
With no start and no end
An 'X' marking each spot of her insecurities.
Once upon a time her mind began to twist, mould and manipulate her
        thoughts
Until it stopped belonging to her and became its own ugly entity
The witch in her fairy tale, trapping her in a castle of her own thoughts
No way out, no way back, no way through.
Solitude and silence became her only friends as she slipped into the
        shadows more and more
Becoming a background character in everyone else's fairytales
As thought after thought and brick after brick sentenced her to a life
        locked within herself
She began to dream and plan.
If she had locked herself in this castle, then surely she could free
        herself too.
Day after day she began to destroy the bricks instead of forming them
Using the rubble to lift herself back into the light
And start to recover herself again.
Time was patient with her.
She didn't live happily ever after, because no one truly does,
There was no fanfare, no celebratory ball, no one else to save her but
        herself
But she recovered what she needed the most: herself.

Seren Delahaye

Convalescence

snow through the fence posts
one crow, one broken branch
the days are too short

the path through the forest blocked by a fallen tree, not one of the
feathered new pines in a too-shallow hole, but the heaviest beech. Soil
still drips from the upended roots, red squirrel boxes lie cracked on the
ground

this spring, only a few of the daffodils bloom, the other bulbs rot,
overwhelmed by the floods

the recovery agent collects what I owe, grabs not only apples released
by the storm, but the glowing ripe fruit which fits in my hands

I dream of a cactus too old to keep growing, not waiting for rain

Shelley Tracey

Remembering

Radiant and resilient
Exuberant and excitable
Creative and curious
Overt and open-hearted
Virtuous and veracious
Eloquent and earnest
Remarkable and reflective

You will always be remembered.

Sonja Miller

Life full Of scars

Karma should have broken me
The Kraken is awake in me
Kaos tries to rule
The Joker and the fool

Keep giving me shit to digest
So I'll find words to manifest
The harder you push it
The harder you detest it
Don't let it deter you.

Don't let ego fool you,
School you, be the true you.
Find the tools to bend the rules
Yours is the way, the path is yours
you've come this far alone.

Down eight stand nine
Wrote ten you're at it again
Shit you've been fed
Compassion in your head.

Standing tall at five foot fuck all
Voice proud words to match
You talk no jest you are at best
When life throws curve balls

Hell stalls we've been in those halls
Fires a passion angers abated
As you stated waited a lifetime
To get this far a life without jars.

A life full of scars.

Spartacus T'ruth

Joint declaration

Misunderstandings, false starts –
two unknowing, broken hearts.
So long ago. All seemed lost
till, years late, the bridge was crossed –
love declared that once was dreamed.
Pain and sadness shared – redeemed.

Steve Dixon

Baptism

I step into the coldness,
first, my left foot, and then my right.
My toes curl against the clammy ground.
I let myself
sink further in.

The black dog laps up my knees, and I let it
happen. Its slobber is far from holy
water. I force myself down.
Immersed by this ocean.

This body of forgiveness.
The first thing I notice is the salt.
Then: the relief, the mercy,
the frailty, the wonder.

Tallulah Howarth

Plant

Since you left
to the land of the
gods
Your precious plant
started to decay
As time passed
I found the strength
to water it
drop by drop
day by day
till it bloomed
again.

Tamara McLorg

In other words

What do you mean by Recovery?
Here's some replies that I've heard.
Recuperation or reconstruction,
Retrieval or a similar word.
Maybe revival or even resurgence,
Repossession, reclamation?
Good suggestions or slightly absurd?
Perhaps it means rebound,
Return, readjustment? Who knows?
To rally or rescue,
Remember, re-think or re-use?
You choose.

Teresa Domene

Battle

January 2021. Emergency admission to hospital. I did not want to go
in.
Covid everywhere – hospital full of it – didn't want to become one of
the many.
Perforated diverticulum meant I had no choice.
Repeatedly tested negative for covid. Finally admitted to the surgical
ward.
Tried to focus on recovery.

Laparoscopy failed. Needed Hartmann's procedure but caught Covid
Acquired Pneumonia.
Moved to a covid ward. Lack of trained staff. People either panicking
or dying.
No visitors. No tv or radio to distract from the hell all around.
Sounds of suffering day and night.
Lights on all the time.
People desperately trying to breathe with their lungs and oxygen
masks failing.
Oxygen mask smothering me.
My PICC lines compromised because no-one available to monitor them
regularly.
Tried to focus on recovery.

Lack of trained medical staff and delay in surgery led to me developing
sepsis.
Told I had less than a 20% chance of survival.
Moved to ICU overflow. Finally, medical staff who knew how to care
for me. Finally, after weeks, I was washed and had my teeth cleaned.
Moved back to covid ward ready for Hartmann's procedure.
Tried to focus on recovery.

Had Hartmann's procedure. Eventually moved back to surgical ward
      after nurses complained about the state I was in. One of them
      cried, saying –
this lady shouldn't be in this condition – we're in a first world
      country, not a third.
Discharged April 2021.
More operations done. More to come.
Still trying to focus on recovery.

Teresa Fox

Charity shop

Excuse me, you've spelled sure *wrong.*
Where?
Above the entrance. Spelt S U E R. It sort of leaps out at you.
Okay, read the whole thing: sueryder.org. It's our website.
Ah, sorry about that. I must have RPB – random perceptual bias.
Even though it's not yet a recognised condition... Is there anything else I can help you with? How are you on semantics, rules of grammar, usage, logic ...?
Generally, ok. Ok...? Or is it OK? Or okay? Hmm, now I'm not sure –
Sure or suer*? Just messin'. If you're thinking of buying a book I can recommend this one:*
How to Survive and Recover from Life's Vicissitudes.
I might be tempted if I knew what a vicissitude was.
Usually plural: ups and downs of life?
Can you give me an example?
Yes, here's one from p34: Dear Marge, help, help, help! I've completed a detailed audit with my clown-therapist and discovered that my life is too full! I spend 26% of my time sleeping, 29% trying to get to sleep, 17% plotting to outwit my energy monitor, and 31% trying to shoo houseflies out of wide-open windows. How can I possibly reduce my activity by 3% – even more if I ever need to get a job?
Wow, I need that book! *How much?*
Reduced to £25. Tell you what, I'll throw in this Fowler's Modern English Usage, given your condition.
Too kind.
Do come again. We definitely need more customers like you.

Terry Buchan

Hydrotherapy in different water

I saw it written as I woke,
on the white board that steers my days.
10:15 am HT with C R. PT.
My PT born in Italy, assigned to mend
the broken, dead side.
She is a proud Paduan, but I
keep thinking of that girl from Bellagio.

Awkward painful slide into bathers.
Danny helps, he teases.
Going swimming today boss
with the lovely Claudia, it's your lucky day.
He gets an uneasy, crooked smile,
think of that summer spent in Como
like now in search of cures for dented dignity.
He whistles pushing me down unfamiliar corridors.

They lift me into strange water,
she is there and I am content.
Holding my hand, we tread the temperate pool.
I feel my feet on the bottom smooth, uncertain,
like the pebbles that day at San Giovanni.
I taste this new water that smarts my lips,
it's tepid, sour, chlorine bleached.

I think of the crisp cool water of the Lago
swimming uncovered at midnight with
the girl from Bellagio.
She gently makes me move my dead side
life returns slowly to morose, morbid limbs,
soft form brushes my arm.
I remember love in Lombardy, drinking Franciacorta
eating *Michetta*, the sweet gift of bees.

She dries my hair, I am back in the chair.
Grazie, mi piace stare in acqua, I tell her.
That's good she says, *that's good,*
let's get you back to the ward,
well done, we'll do it again.

Tim Brookes

Mr C

Yo mr C I don't love you anymore

Started with a key and now ma nose it feeling sore

With every other line it's fucking burning and it's raw

Now it's flipping bleeding dripping claret in the floor

But the high will never be as good as before

Yo the high will never be as good as before

We got a love hate relationship and I ain't about no wasting shit so am a finish the whole bag even if it is basic sniff

Basically what am tryna say is that am hating it, I literally despise every line even if it's amazing whiff, Amazingly it never is

Even the good stuff is devilish

Devils dandruff turns ya devil and makes you pretty dangerous

Changes ya personality now your characters some shady prick

Scrapping round a bag that made some lad beaten rich, cut and mixed eight times before it reaches you, So what's it made with kid?

Benzocane, Hence the blame and a whole load of other names, You call the dealer but call the dealer a thousand names but who's to blame? Their just making their drink and their cut, it's you that should be ashamed cos this really is a mugs game

But you keep going, ya nose is snowing

Mr know it all? Yeah I know it

Spoken word or broken verbs

Broke down emotions and coke up nerves

Anxiety's on suicide watch and the come down never seems to come down and come up's so fast it hurts

And then it's over in a flash, the day that turned to night is in the past

Just left with a heavy head full of thoughts and the sound of your own heart beat beat against ya chest birds singing to the beat but you can't beat this feeling

You're depressed

Tommy Too Shugs

Uncovering the past at the Ness of Brodgar

Some of the objects found hidden in the nooks and crannies of those ancient buildings were, we think, offerings to their gods. Not intended for us. We recognise this, treat them with reverence and awe. The polished stone axes, carved stone balls, the odd human thigh bone, the incised stones with their butterfly and zigzag motifs, carry meanings far beyond our comprehension and modern sensibilities. But other things recovered from this site are a mix of lost and discarded things: broken pots, cow bones, flint scrapers, arrow heads, tiny spatulas and beads. The detritus of everyday life. We study them, probe and pry with eyes, hands, and all the scientific tests and machines we have today. We seek out meaning, peer through a dense veil of time at the people who lived here, five thousand years ago. Sometimes we get close, just for a moment; the thumb print of a potter, the paw print of a dog, the imprint of a woven mat, captured on wet clay.

Tonnie Richmond

Embers of resilience

In the depths of darkness, I once lay still,
A battle-scarred warrior, worn and chill.
Cancer's grasp had left its mark,
A howling of fear, a shadow in the dark.

But even as the fire raged within,
A spark within me refused to give in.
A flame of hope, a glimmer of light,
Guided me through the darkest of nights.

The treatment's heat, a burning pain,
A path of trial, a road to regain.
Radiation's waves crashed, a turbulent sea,
But I rode the tides, steadfast and free.

With each new dawn, a chance to begin,
To rediscover life, to let love back in
The embers of resilience they still glowed bright,
I rose again, stronger, wiser, in the light.

For cancer may have taken its toll,
This time it couldn't claim my soul.
I've learned to cherish every breath,
To savour each moment, and not to fear my death.

So let my story be a beacon bright,
A guiding light for those who still face the fight.
Know that you are strong, that you are brave,
And though the journey's hard, you can rise above the wave.

Tony Dawson

Dust-covered radio shows recovered
for Dusty

Testing... one, two, three...
Is anyone out there? Can you hear us?

...We are the recovered radio shows,
born in this happy place. Home from the future.

We shook off that dusty-old-dust.
We seeped out of Seacroft.
We outlasted the collapse of Chapel FM.

We survived the pop-up empires
and humankind cluttering & muttering of this isle.

We made it out, out into the draughty old cosmos.

We are coming back, to your ears, now –
radio shows from beyond the Oort Cloud, light years.
If you get the itch, even you
can eavesdrop-in on us.

It is difficult
to get the news from archives
– a gentle jolt, a tap on the shoulder
from a lost friend. Yet –

To recover our radio waves, follow these nimble instructions:

1. *Disable all inessential ear-aches and listener-pains.*
2. *Back up your wistfulness and panic periodically.*
3. *Upgrade to version 6.2 of curiosity (cat, homo-sapien, or other species).*
4. *Do not peel apples or other fruit while feeling tone is rebooting.*

5. *Compress any melancholy to fit facial-expression file format size.*
6. *If dust (star- or other sort) accumulates, gently wipe sound archive counter-clockwise.*
7. *Repeat 1-6 until fully in-tune.*

Are we live now? Have you found the frequency?
Someone to witness and adjust the dial!

Tony Macaluso

The monkeys are stealing my spoons

Measuring energy levels in spoons is a fatigue management technique. A monkey on your back i.e. problems, is a drain on energy.

The monkeys are stealing my spoons.
It's a never-ending juggling act.
The problem is I need the spoons to balance the monkeys.

I wouldn't mind but I never had a full set of spoons to start off with.
I feel permanently exhausted, just getting up uses spoons.

However, sometimes a joyful monkey will come along bringing spoons.
I devour them.
Their joy permeating my soul.

I saw my friend today.
She was in a bad way.
Monkeys climbing all over her.
I took one off her.
I saw the spoons transfer to her but she did give me one back.
I know she'd do the same for me.
Friends share monkeys.
That's how you defeat them – monkeys not friends of course.

The monkeys have stolen all my spoons.
Now I'm forced to recover in bed while the monkeys chase each other
through my mind.
I must rest up, charge my batteries.
I must get some more spoons.

I'm my own worst enemy.
Sometimes I positively invite the monkeys onboard.
I just can't say no.
Life is an adventure.
Who knows where my monkeys will take me.

Now this looks like a promising little monkey.
Deadline tomorrow.
No problem, hop onboard.

Vickie Orton

Answers to FAQs

Where do I find the quarterly statistics for the number of bed days spent by 0-17 year-olds on adult wards in 2017?

Where can I find the monthly statistics for the number of physical restraints involving people with learning disabilities in England in the financial years 2012-2013, and 2013-2014?

Where can I find the number of patients currently in contact with mental health services whose accommodation status is *homeless*?

Where can I find the number of patients currently in contact with mental health services who have served in HM Forces?

Where can I find the total number of patients in contact with mental health services, broken down by age?

Where can I find the number of Inappropriate Out of Area Placements which were more than 200 kilometres away from the patient's local contact area?

Where can I find the number of patients with a diagnosis of *gender dysmorphia*, who also have a diagnosis of *self-harm*, broken down by *gender at birth*?

How many patients with a diagnosis category of *common disorder* in the last 12 months were in employment, and had an accommodation status in the *mainstream housing* group? Where can I find them?

You can find them in every city and town, in every human settlement.

You can find them in every workplace, on every street corner. Not all are holding out empty paper cups.

Some of us write books.

William Thirsk Gaskill

Spring cleaning

I've always been hesitant to let people in further than the hallway. There are dirty dishes in the sink and shattered glass on the floor and fear hangs in the corners like spiderwebs. Fear of you leaving more fallout in your steps or fear of you leaving bloody footprints, or both.

I don't want you to walk on eggshells but I need you to tread carefully and I'm not sure how to reconcile the two.

Maybe I just need more time to sort out this mess and I know you'll be right there with cake and some incense to air out the fog. And we'll lie in bed and watch the sun set and rise and won't even notice. There is still glass on the floor but I can see it clearly now in the light on your face and I sweep it up while you sweep me off my feet. Pulling the shards out of my skin is easier in the safety of your arms.

I don't need your bandages but I treasure your hand in mine while I'm dressing my own wounds.

Wren Aster

Canal side recovery

Brenda preferred to paddleboard along the canal in the morning, peacefully and with the freshness of a new day. She adjusted her balance as she approached a family of swans. She could only imagine the eye-roll her physiotherapist would give if whilst recovering from the hit and run she was taken down by a swan. This family seemed to have an understanding with her though after she had helped disentangle the mother from a discarded fishing line. It had opened Brenda's eyes to the litter people would drop in this little bit of paradise. The water may be murkier than a true-blue sea, but the canals were veins of life still. Fish swimming around, the quacking of paddling ducks. The majesty of a statue-still heron, waiting to pounce. The darting emerald flashes of dragonflies. Even the honking of geese, who always sounded angry, had become familiarly reassuring between the chugging of brightly coloured canal barges. Paddleboarding had helped rebuild her physical strength, challenged her and more importantly, chased away some of the blues that had plagued her since the accident.

Brenda helped the canal recover as she did with her waterway litter-picking. She had accepted recovery was not a checklist to blast through or easily predictable. More of a journey. She had decided to embrace the process and she – and the canal – were both doing a lot better for it. Brenda paddled on, seeing what else she would see today and feeling calm about the uncertainty.

Yvonne Lang

The losing game

He staggered up the grassy verge
Ensnared within a dream
A living, hellish nightmare
Just a boy of seventeen
His hollow cheeks were pale and drawn
His glassy eyes so dim
I knew the game he'd tried to play
A fight he'd never win
He slowly slumped against the wall
His shaking hands employed
In checking out the deadly drugs
That made his young life void
I saw the needle in his arm
A face that knew no shame
Eyes that lit with joy
To see the poison flood his vein
The deed now done, he closed his eyes
With rainbows in his mind
The night was cold, his clothes were thin
How can we be so blind?
I felt the tears upon my face
And sought for reasons why
– I cradled him within my arms
Afraid to watch him die
What can we do to stop this hell?
Will no-one heed his call?
Why do we STILL refuse to read
The writing on the wall?
He died upon that grassy verge
Ensnared within a dream
Without the love the world should give
To boys of seventeen

Yvonne Ugarte

Biographies

Abigail Ottley writes poetry and short fiction. A Pushcart and Best of the Net nominee, twice winner of the Wildfire 150, she came second in the 2024 Plaza Prose Poetry competition.

Adrian Salmon lives in Bingley, West Yorkshire. His pamphlet, *Moonlight through the Velux window*, was published in June 2019 by Yaffle Press.

Alex Callaghan is a non-binary poet from Yorkshire and an editor for Written Off Publishing who specialise in nonsense and the absurd.

Ali Murphy has had poems published in *High Window, Black Nore, Ink Sweat and Tears, Dawntreader, Bread and Roses*, Leeds Festival anthology, Yaffle anthologies and won 2nd prize in Wakefield Red Shed.

Angie Smiles is an actor, soprano and comic. She volunteers as a Legal Advisor for Citizens Advice when not busy writing.

Ann Clarke writes to entertain herself but is delighted when it works for other people. A member of Leeds Writers' Circle, she has been a regular contributor to The Deli.

Ann Heath lives and works in York. She has most recently been published in *Atrium, Black Nore Review, The Lake* and *Ink, Sweat and Tears*.

Aqeel Parvez is a poet from Bradford. His 12th chapbook *Silks Of Assai* (Backroom Poetry, 2024) is out now.

Ben Grunwell is a 17-year-old Flemish-influenced writer from Leeds, unpublished until now. He has appeared on Channel 4's Countdown.

Billy Myers says, *I'm 25 years old and have Asperger's Syndrome. I've been writing at Chapel FM for a number of years which gives me the opportunity to develop my creativity and share it with other like-minded people.*

Bryan Jayden Muzambi is a young enthusiastic wordsmith at Chapel FM who enjoys using his imagination, day to day life experiences and creativity to inspire his writing.

Biographies

Carmel Gibbons taught in the classroom for 32 years. She runs the business *Writing Matters* and teaches creative writing online to children and adults, describing herself as a budding poet, musician and lifetime observer of nature.

Catherine Lynn Kirby has always enjoyed the creative arts, especially dancing and writing, and hopes to repeat the success of this much appreciated opportunity to be heard.

Chalky The Punk is a member of The Chapel FM Writing Group.

Chris O'Connor is a Leeds playwright who has written for Leeds Playhouse, BBC Radio and Red Ladder. This is his first foray into writing poetry and he is honoured to have it published here.

Colin Day is a poet and proud member of the Yaffle/Wordship family who is surprised to find that all his poems are like children whom he loves indiscriminately and without judgement.

Cora Greenhill finds her best writing often arises from being discombobulated by travel, or by imaginatively travelling to past eras: her most recent book is set in ancient Crete.

Dalton Harrison is a dyslexic queer poet. After leaving prison he found his creative home at Chapel FM. *The Boy Behind The Wall* is his first poetry collection.

David Annwn's 14th poetry collection, *Wonder-rig* (with Lee Duggan) was published last year.

David Harmer lives in Doncaster and publishes poetry for children and grown-ups. Chapel FM have been kind enough to invite him onto Love the Words a few times.

Eleanor May Blackburn is a 27-year-old actor/writer whose first pamphlet was released by Cerasus in 2021. Her first full collection is due from Stairwell in 2025.

Ellie Thompson says *Writing creates a sense of freedom without the pressures of society. It has played a large role in who I have become.*

Emmy battles chronic pain to write short stories and flash fiction at Chapel FM. She hopes to publish a collection and even write a full-length novel or two.

115

Biographies

Gail Mosley has always loved poetry but began writing after retiring from teaching. She found inspiration with the help of the WEA, Leeds Playhouse Heydays and Barney Bardsley's Wordplay.

Gareth Rhodes is a writer from Leeds who, looking inward and outward, tries to do his best. He's contributed many poems and stories to Chapel FM and highly recommends that you do too.

Garry Cochrane is a sometime poet and writer, with an unpublished debut novel in his top drawer. He has a fascination with Ernest Hemingway which, oddly enough, encouraged him to stop drinking.

Gill Connors lives, writes and swims near the Dales in North Yorkshire. She is working on a third collection of poems.

Hannah Stone is a Leeds writer who collaborates with other poets and composers and has been widely published. She edits *Dream Catcher* journal.

Hans-Ulrich Heuser lives in Hagen in Germany and likes Dadaism and Surrealism. He prefers writing short form poems, stories and plays.

Helen Rice is a writer and performer based in Sheffield. She won Leeds Poetry Festival's competition in 2022 and her debut pamphlet *I'm Not Your Mother* is published by Written Off.

Helen Shay is a Yorkshire writer, who has worked with Chapel FM since Boggart Hill days on plays ranging from a Dracula spoof to one featuring the Chapel's in situ organ.

Hilary Robinson writes lyric, sometimes experimental, poetry about lived experiences and dreams. Her joint collection with Rachel Davies about dementia is out this autumn.

Holly Bars lives in Leeds. Her debut collection, *Dirty*, is published with Yaffle Press.

Jacqui Ambler helps run a 26-acre cemetery in Bradford. In her spare time she enjoys writing and sharing poetry at various venues in Bradford, including Sisterhood open mic at City Library.

Jaimes Lewis Moran is an Autistic Poet proudly hailing from Seacroft, East Leeds. Passionate about electric skateboards, Jaimes has published six themed collections of poetry.

Biographies

James Fernie is a long-time member of The Deli writing group. A dyed-in-the-wool Hippie who refuses to grow up, his love of travel, new experiences and people often inspires his writing.

Jaspreet Mander is a Yorkshire-based full-time writer. Her work, verse and prose, has been published in magazines and anthologies.

Jennifer A. McGowan is a multiply-disabled poet. Her last collection, *How to be a Tarot Card (or a Teenager)*, is available from Arachne Press.

Joan Bosomworth lives near Otley and is often inspired by this beautiful area. She grew up in Bradford and many happy memories are reflected in her WordPlay pieces.

Josie Walsh, planning a fourth collection, has read her work on Chapel FM and Radio 4. For a decade she edited *Under Glass*, a community poetry magazine at Pugneys where she still walks, often writing in her head.

Julia Deakin is widely published, with four collections and a fifth imminent. She edits *Pennine Platform* and has read on BBC Radio 4 – but nothing beats working with Chapel FM.

Julie Griffiths is a poet from Sheffield, who now lives in Wales. Her work has been published through Penned on the Bont and Yaffle's Nest. She is currently working on her debut pamphlet.

Kay Boardman writes and produces children's poetry books from her home in the hilltops above Hebden Bridge, West Yorkshire.

Keith Fenton is a poet, event host, historian, podcaster and MA student who presents and produces Sports Talk and contributes to The Deli and other shows on East Leeds Community Radio.

Leeds East Academy is the closest school to Chapel FM geographically. All the featured poets have been members of the writing group Peter Spafford facilitates at the school.

Linda Casper is a retired teacher and wannabe novelist. She is part of the team who present The Deli, a regular radio programme at Chapel FM, for which she writes flash fiction, poetry and plays.

Biographies

Linda Marshall regularly manifests at the Chapel FM writing group sessions. She has four poetry collections to her name and, who knows, another may materialise some day.

Linn Schiffmann is a non-binary artist and writer from Dortmund. They like to blend literature and visual art to amplify LGBTQ voices.

Lisa Falshaw lives and works in West Yorkshire and has had poems published by *Black Bough*, *Atrium*, *Dreamcatcher*, *Dawn Treader*, *Strix*, *Fig Tree*, *Fevers of the Mind*, *Orbis* and *Ink Sweat and Tears*.

Liz Dawson is a member of the Chapel FM Writing Group and of the storytelling sessions, which have helped her overcome her lack of confidence due to dyslexia.

Liz McPherson's work has been published in online and print. She was runner up in the Poetry Society Stanza Competition in 2021 and shortlisted for the Leeds Peace Poetry Prize in 2024.

Lydia Kennaway has an MA in Writing Poetry from Newcastle University. Her poetry pamphlet *A History of Walking* was published by HappenStance Press in 2019.

Madeleine Andrews finds the Wordplay sessions an enriching experience, *especially because you hear how other people's imaginations work.*

Madeleine Wuidart was inspired by James Brunt's 'Coastal Ecologies' exhibition in Scarborough. An autistic artist and writer, her creativity is nurtured by immersion in nature.

Mally Harvey, after a lifelong love affair with the spoken and written word, has been encouraged to share her work through Heydays, Shine magazine, Chapel FM, Leeds library and WordPlay.

Mandy Schiffrin is half-British, half-Argentinian. She lives and works in the Netherlands. She has had poetry published in several publications, online and in print.

Marg Greenwood is a writer of prose, poems and songs, with many published articles in magazines. Her recent book *Return to Muck* recounts her solo travels in lesser-known Scottish islands.

Margaret Bending is a member of The Performance Ensemble and of the writing group Wordplay, run by Barney Bardsley.

Biographies

Mark Connors is a widely published novelist, poet and creative writing facilitator from Leeds. He is the co-managing editor at Yaffle and Yaffle's Nest.

Mary Cooper (Senior) co-wrote the ground-breaking *Growing Old Disgracefully*, as well as its sequel. Formerly a lecturer, Mary recently celebrated her 100th birthday.

Matt Nicholson is a poet and performer from East Yorkshire. His work has a dark, urgent and cynical energy to it.

Michael Hassell is an actor/performer with the Performance Ensemble and other local community theatre groups. He would like to write stories and drama for the radio.

Mick Robinson has been attending the Orb writing group for a few years. He likes being creative, especially when it comes to avoiding chores.

Nancy Elwell joined Chapel FM in January 2024. Since retiring she enjoys having time to pursue her interest in writing, honing her skills and technique.

Neil Rathmell grew up in Horsforth. He has been widely published, his most recent work being *Dorothy* (Valley Press, 2023), a true story told in verse.

Newton Albrecht is a strange little man who haunts Orb in Knaresborough and writes because he is plagued by visions of queer joy. He has too many craft hobbies and a mildly-concerning puppet fascination.

Nicki Powell says, *I'm new to writing and enjoying trying out different styles and subject matter. This is the first step towards my ambition to write a book!*

Nicola Good is a language activist, teacher and writer. She ran school projects in Chapel FM's festival for the 50th anniversary of the Leeds-Dortmund twinning.

Oz Hardwick has won many prizes, mostly for pub quizzes but occasionally for poetry. His most recent chapbook is *Retrofuturism for the Dispossessed* (Hedgehog, 2024). Oz is Professor of Creative Writing at Leeds Trinity University.

Biographies

Pen Kease, who has an MA in Writing from Warwick University and is widely published, has released her first collection, *This Side of the Sea*, now available through Yaffle Press.

Penny Blackburn is a Yorkshire-born writer now living in the North East. She continues to take inspiration from her roots and experiences.

Pete Tidy is a dramaturg and scriptwriter inspired by John Godber, Lemn Sissay, Peter Cook, Eniola Aluko and Nick Hornby, who devises, directs and performs improvised Theatre-in-Education.

Peter McDonagh has been writing for recovery as a way to develop his voice. For anyone continuing to develop as a writer, he would advocate lifelong learning strategies through informal and formal courses.

Rachel Clark-Wilson is a mindfulness teacher and Reiki healer who sometimes gathers words. She finds inspiration, joy and wisdom for life in nature. This is her first published piece.

Rachel Davies's greatest achievement is being mother, grandmother and great grandmother. A very close second is being a widely-published poet.

Rachel Flint believes that writing poetry declutters the mind. She advocates connecting with nature as a means of healing.

Ralf Thenior lives in Dortmund, Germany. Poet, allotment gardener and night-botanist, friend of Leeds and Chapel FM, Ralf yearns to see the Yorkshire Dales again.

Robert Hill has written off and on over the years. *In Calverley Street* is his first published poem.

Sandra Burnett values her many programmes with Otley Poets for Chapel FM's Writing on Air Festivals. For inspiration she moseys around local backroads on her electric bike.

Sarah Rooke, aka Worrier Queen uses spoken word with love, passion and humour to share her personal story, thoughts and wisdom gleaned as a survivor of 32 years of domestic abuse.

Seren Delahaye is 16 and an avid reader, writer and creative. She's participated in various groups at Chapel FM since 2020 and hopes to use the skills she's developed here to pursue a career in writing.

Biographies

Shelley Tracey is a South African poet who lives in Northern Ireland. Shelley's poems have been published in many journals and in her collection *Elements of Distance* (Lapwing, 2017).

Sonja Miller, a retired Head of Expressive Arts, enjoys her involvement with Chapel FM along with volunteering, playing tennis, and being involved in community dance.

At 16 in the British Army, Steve Parkins (**Spartacus T'ruth**) was being trained to kill. That made him Unwell. At nearly 50 he found solace in Poetry.

Steve Dixon is a retired education adviser. He has had poetry, short stories and scripts published, performed and anthologised.

Tallulah Howarth is a multidisciplinary artist studying an MA in Writing Poetry at Newcastle University. They are particularly passionate about foraging, archives and Polish jazz.

Tamara McLorg is a member of WordPlay run by Barney Bardsley, and of The Performance Ensemble.

Teresa Domene loves cats, most people, blue skies, Valencia and reading.

Teresa Fox battles PTSD, IBD and constant pain by accessing varied support that includes Orb, a charity based in Knaresborough. She has self-published a children's book, *Hogey, the Birthday Dragon*.

Terry Buchan was involved in Leeds Comedy Writers Forum until it went extinct, shortly after all the members espoused Northern Darwinism. He writes for the Deli programme at Chapel FM

Tim Brookes has lived in Yorkshire most of his life. He used to teach but now helps run a food bank and Getting Gobby in the Lobby spoken word night.

Tommy Too Shugs is a spoken word artist from Manchester. Inspiration for his poetry comes from real life experiences, particularly of own mental health struggles.

Tonnie Richmond lives in Leeds, loves Orkney and archaeology, and has had many poems published. Her pamphlet, *Rear-view Mirror*, was published by Yaffle's Nest in 2023.

Biographies

Tony Dawson is a musician, lighting technician and mainstay of East Leeds Dramatic Arts (ELDA) who rehearse and perform regularly at Chapel FM.

Tony Macaluso is the author of theatre plays, a book on Chicago music history, chapters on radio and oral historian Studs Terkel, and is Director of Chapel FM Arts Centre.

Vickie Orton is an oral storyteller and has been writing stories and poems for as long as she can remember. She regularly tells stories on East Leeds Community Radio.

William Thirsk-Gaskill is a member of Black Horse Poets in Wakefield, and has had a play produced on BBC Radio 4. In 2024 he organised Writing For Wellbeing, an event sponsored by Wakefield Council.

Wren Aster is a writer, photographer and organiser of the Queer Poetry Gala in her hometown of Dortmund, Germany. They often appear on Queer stages in the Rhine-Ruhr area.

Yvonne Lang is a Yorkshire based writer who loves creating stories of all genres. She is an expert at typing around a cat with no respect for personal space.

Yvonne Ugarte has been writing poetry since the age of five. Her last book raised over £1,000 for Martin House Children's Hospice.

Also published by YAFFLE Press

Fairground	Penny Sharman	£6.50
The Magpie's Box	Terry Simpson	£6.50
Tadaima	Gill Lambert	£9.00
Whirlagust	Various	£9.00
All of the Moons	Mike Farren	£6.50
Moonlight through the Velux Window	Adrian Salmon	£6.50
Wilderness of Skin	Kathleen Strafford	£9.00
Quotidian	Paul Waring	£6.50
Reel Bradford	Yaffle 5	£10.00
Optics	Mark Connors	£10.00
Only Blood	Pat Edwards	£6.50
Pandemonium	Keith Lander	£6.50
And the Stones Fell Open	Various	£10.00
An Insubstantial Universe	Various	£10.00
Small Havocs	Matt Nicholson	£10.00
Enchanter's Nightshade	Simon Currie	£10.00
Fiery Daughters	Lorna Faye Dunsire	£6.50
Bloody Amazing	Various	£10.00
Whirlagust II	Various	£10.00
Cloud Cuckoo Café	Linda Marshall	£10.00
Learning from the Body	Sue Butler	£6.50
Symmetry of Folklore	Donna Irving	£7.00
Frisk	Peter Spafford	£10.00
Forged	Tina Cole	£7.00
Hi-Viz	Ben Banyard	£10.00
After	Mark Connors	£10.00
Untanglement	Matt Nicholson	£10.00
A Small Goodbye at Dawn	Gill Lambert	£10.00
The Doll's Hospital	Jenny Robb	£10.00
Whirlagust III	Various	£10.00

The Invisible Woman	Lesley Quayle	£10.00
Dirty	Holly Bars	£10.00
Duff	Various	£10.00
The Last Almanac	Bob Beagrie	£12.00
A to Z of Superstitions	Ian Harker	£7.00
Gaps Made of Static	Penny Blackburn	£10.00
Whirlagust IV	Various	£10.00
Missing	Various	£5.00
Girl in the Woods	Kathleen Strafford	£12.00
The Weight of Blood	Bobbie Sparrow	£12.00
This Side of the Sea	Pen Kease	£12.00
Hear the World Explode	Jenny Robb	£12.00
Held	Kevin Reid	£12.00

Please go to https://www.yafflepress.co.uk/shop to purchase any of the above titles.